THE 12 MOST AMAZING
AMERICAN MYTHS & LEGENDS

by Anita Yasuda

12 STORY LIBRARY

www.12StoryLibrary.com

12-Story Library is an imprint of Peterson Publishing Company and Press Room Editions.

Produced for 12-Story Library by Red Line Editorial

Photographs ©: Louella938/Shutterstock Images, cover, 1; Ron and Joe/Shutterstock Images, 4, 28; AP Images, 5, 17; Currier & Ives/Library of Congress, 6; Detroit Publishing Co./Library of Congress, 7, 11; Elise Amendola/AP Images, 8; Michael Garland/Peterson Publishing Company, 9, 23; Carol M. Highsmith/Library of Congress, 10; Digital Paws Inc./Thinkstock, 12; C. Stuart/Library of Congress, 13; Bettmann/Corbis, 15, 27; R.K. Fox/Library of Congress, 16; Jean Leon Gerome Ferris/Library of Congress, 18, 29; Olivier Le Queinec/Shutterstock Images, 19; Tom Grundy/Shutterstock Images, 20; Neftali/Shutterstock Images, 21; AlexanderZam/Shutterstock Images, 22; Daniel M. Silva/Shutterstock Images, 24; Steven Wynn/Thinkstock, 25

ISBN
978-1-63235-010-7 (hardcover)
978-1-63235-070-1 (paperback)
978-1-62143-051-3 (hosted ebook)

Library of Congress Control Number: 2014937245

9-1-15

Printed in the United States of America
Mankato, MN
June, 2014

STORY
LIBRARY

Go beyond the book. Get free, up-to-date content on this topic at 12StoryLibrary.com.

TABLE OF CONTENTS

JOHN HENRY BECOMES FAMOUS FOR RACING MACHINE

John Henry was known as the strongest man on the railroad. According to storytellers, he could knock down a mountain with a hammer. Some historians think the African-American folk hero was based on a real man who was born in the 1840s or 1850s as a slave. After the Civil War, he went to work for the C&O Railroad. As a steel driver, his job was to pound on a steel spike or drill with a hammer. Then workers put explosives in the drill hole to blast away the rock.

The real John Henry was said to be among approximately 1,000 workers who dug a passageway through Big Bend Mountain. The men chipped away at the mountain for three years. The work was so difficult, hundreds of them died. Henry was known as the strongest and most powerful man on the job.

According to legend, Henry could cut through 10 to 20 feet (3 to 6 m) of rock in a 12-hour workday. One day a salesman brought a new

Railroad workers in the late 1800s told John Henry's story for inspiration.

steam-powered drill to the tunnel. Henry raced the machine to see who could cut through the rock the fastest. He won. He died shortly afterward from exhaustion. But his story lived on. Railroad workers sang about John Henry as they worked. His strength was an inspiration. In the years since, stories about John Henry's life have been told in books, plays, films, and songs.

Singer Paul Robeson played the title role in the 1940 musical *John Henry*.

400

Approximate number of recordings of a song about John Henry that have been made.

- Possibly based on a real African-American railroad worker.
- Helped dig the Big Bend tunnel in West Virginia in the 1870s.
- Known for winning a race against a steam-powered drill.

LEGENDS

A legend is a kind of story that is passed down. Some legends are believed to be based on a real person or event. Parts of the story may contain true facts. Other parts have been made up or exaggerated. Sometimes it is difficult to tell which parts of a legend are true and which are made up.

2

STORMALONG HAS ADVENTURES ON THE HIGH SEAS

According to New England folklore, Alfred Bulltop Stormalong was the best sailor in the world. Stormy, as he was called, was a giant man. He tied sea monsters into knots.

In the late 1800s, sailors sang songs about Stormy while they worked. These songs were called chanteys. The character in the songs was always brave and bold.

Stormy's ship, the *Courser*, was based on clipper ships like this one.

One myth about Alfred Bulltop Stormalong explains how the cliffs of Dover, England, became white.

In the 1930s, writer Frank Shay put Stormy into a book. It was called *Here's Audacity*. Shay's Stormy could blow a ship home with one breath. In later versions, the sails of his giant ship, the *Courser*, could knock the sun out of the sky.

According to one story, Stormy once tried to sail the *Courser* through the English Channel. The *Courser* was so wide that the crew had to rub its sides with soap. That way it wouldn't get stuck. The soap scraped off the sides of the ship onto the cliffs of Dover. That's how the cliffs became white, the story goes.

24

Height in feet (7 m) of Captain Stormalong, according to legend.

- Fictional sea captain from New England folklore.
- Sailed on the *Courser*, the largest ship ever built.
- First appeared in a sea song called "Stormalong."

MYTHS

A myth is an old story that has been told and retold for many years. Some myths express important values in the culture that gives rise to them. Sometimes a myth is used to explain a practice, belief, or natural occurrence. Traditionally, myths were not written down.

PECOS BILL RIDES A TORNADO IN TALL TALES

Cowboy superhero Pecos Bill used a rattlesnake for a lasso. He could ride any horse in Texas. Sometimes, he rode a mountain lion. Once, he even took a ride on a tornado. And it wasn't just any tornado, but the biggest tornado anyone had ever seen.

Pecos Bill was the creation of storytellers. Cowboys told stories about this frontier hero with supernatural abilities for entertainment. These were called tall tales. In 1917, journalist Edward O'Reilly started writing some of these stories down. They were printed in *Century Magazine*. In O'Reilly's version, Pecos Bill was raised by coyotes before learning how to be a cowboy. He was so tough that bullets bounced right off his skin. His horse, named Widow-Maker, ate dynamite.

A series of stamps in 1995 featured legendary characters, including Pecos Bill.

THINK ABOUT IT

A tall tale is a story where unbelievable events are told as if they are true. Why do you think people tell tall tales?

9

Years Edward O'Reilly and Jack Warren coauthored a comic strip about Pecos Bill, from 1929 to 1938.

- Fictional cowboy of the Old West.
- Originated in stories during the 1800s.
- First written about by Edward O'Reilly in 1917.

Pecos Bill is one of the most famous tall tale heroes of the Wild West.

Other writers added to these tall tales. According to one, Pecos Bill fell in love with Slue-Foot Sue. She was riding a giant fish down a river. To impress her, he used his rifle to shoot out all the stars in the sky but one. He called it the Lone Star. While none of the stories are true, people enjoy retelling them. Pecos Bill became a symbol of the old Wild West.

PAUL BUNYAN GROWS INTO LEGENDARY GIANT

As a lumberjack, Paul Bunyan could crush entire forests with one swing of his ax. He dug the Great Lakes as watering holes for his pet ox. His booming voice could make tree branches fall.

Loggers started telling tall tales about Paul Bunyan in the 1880s. Older lumberjacks would tell the stories to new recruits to see if they would believe them. The hero of these early stories was big and strong. He towered seven feet (2.1 m) tall. He represented the values of working hard and overcoming obstacles. James MacGillivray and others started

Statues of the legendary lumberjack Paul Bunyan and his blue ox, Babe, stand in Klamath, California.

publishing the stories around 1910. More Americans heard about the Paul Bunyan stories through advertisements for a logging company.

As Paul Bunyan became a national folk hero, the stories about him became more fantastic. Some said Paul Bunyan was so big, he used a pine tree as a comb. His heavy footprints formed lakes. He traveled with a giant blue ox named Babe. The ox was so strong that it could tug on one end of a road and straighten all the curves. Over the years, Paul Bunyan and Babe have appeared in songs, art, and children's stories. Even poets such as Robert Frost and Carl Sandberg have written about the giant lumberjack.

1,000
Approximate number of books that have mentioned Paul Bunyan.

- Stories originated in the 1880s or earlier.
- Popular among loggers in Wisconsin, Pennsylvania, and the Northwest.
- James MacGillivray was among the first to write down the stories around 1910.

Loggers started telling Paul Bunyan stories in the 1800s for entertainment.

5

DAVY CROCKETT REIGNS OVER THE FRONTIER

Davy Crockett was known as the king of the Wild West. Storytellers said he could leap the Ohio River and carry a steamboat on his back. He appeared in books and plays starting in the 1800s. The character battled wildcats with his bare hands. He killed bears with a single shot. In the 1950s, his stories became the subjects of television shows and films. His image was put on shoes, shirts, and lunch boxes. Children

began wearing coonskin caps like his.

The character from the legends was loosely based on a real person. The real David Crockett did not fight snakes or jump on alligators. Born in 1786, Crockett grew up in Tennessee. He served as a military scout before entering politics. Crockett was elected to the Tennessee legislature in 1821. He also served in the US House of

Coonskin caps like Davy Crockett's became popular in the 1950s.

Representatives for three terms. Another politician called him the "gentleman from the cane." He was referring to the Tennessee wilderness where Crockett hunted bears and raccoons. Based on his rugged image, people started telling wild stories about Crockett.

Crockett's fame increased after he moved to Texas in 1835. He helped the Texans in their fight for independence. Crockett was killed in 1836 at the Battle of the Alamo.

An 1839 portrait shows David Crockett, the frontiersman that Davy Crockett stories are based on.

7 million

Approximate copies of the song "The Ballad of Davy Crockett" sold in the first six months of 1955.

- Based on David Crockett, 1786–1836.
- Portrayed as the ultimate frontier hero.
- Inspired books, television shows, and movies.

COONSKIN CAPS

In the 1950s, the television show *Davy Crockett* set off a fad. Millions of children began wearing coonskin caps. The caps were made from real or fake raccoon fur. Kids wanted to look like the character in the show. At the show's peak, 5,000 caps were sold per day.

JOHNNY APPLESEED SPROUTS STORIES OF KINDNESS

Johnny Appleseed was a new type of frontier hero. He was not known for his strength or his courage. He carried a bag of apple seeds on his back instead of a weapon. He planted apple trees across America.

Johnny Appleseed was actually John Chapman, who lived from 1774 to 1845. Legends paint him as a wanderer who planted seeds wherever he went. But John Chapman was a businessman. He grew seedlings and sold them for profit. He sold thousands of seedlings to pioneers. They planted them to make apple orchards. They used the apples as a food source and to make cider.

Over the years, his character was featured in many songs, plays, and tales. According to one story,

BUSINESS ATTIRE

The real John Chapman dressed in rags and preferred being barefoot. He had long hair and wore a pan on his head like a hat. He cut armholes in a coffee sack to wear as a shirt. Settlers sometimes offered to let him sleep in their cabins. But he preferred to sleep outdoors.

Johnny built a fire in a log. To his surprise, he found bear cubs inside it. He put the fire out and slept in the cold. These stories were based on Chapman's reputation. He was known for being cheerful, generous, and gentle with animals. Although he was running a business, he sometimes gave away seedlings for free to struggling pioneer families.

THINK ABOUT IT

Johnny Appleseed is celebrated in stories for his kindness and generosity. Other legends feature strong or hard-working characters. What traits do you think a hero should have?

1,200

Approximate number of planted acres (480 ha) owned by John Chapman.

- Based on John Chapman, 1774–1845.
- Celebrated for being kind and generous.
- Featured in songs, stories, and plays.

An old children's book illustration shows Johnny Appleseed planting apple trees in the wilderness.

ANNIE OAKLEY SHOOTS INTO STARDOM

Annie Oakley was a real person. And unlike some legendary characters, many of her amazing feats were real. With her rifle, Oakley could shoot the edge of a playing card from 30 paces away. She could shoot a dime tossed up into the air. She could shoot an apple off her dog's head or the flame off a candle. Oakley did all this and more as the star of Buffalo Bill's Wild West show.

Born in 1860 in Ohio, Oakley's real name was Phoebe Ann Mosey. Mosey taught herself to fire a gun

The real Annie Oakley, pictured in 1899

BUFFALO BILL

Buffalo Bill's real name was William Cody. He was a buffalo hunter, army scout, soldier, and performer. In 1883, he started Buffalo Bill's Wild West show. The show featured sharpshooters, trick riders, and live animals such as buffalo and bears. It ran for 30 years, with performances all over the world.

The musical *Annie Get Your Gun* premiered on Broadway in 1946.

at a young age. She hunted quail to help support her family. When she was 15, Mosey won a shooting competition against a famous marksman. People were fascinated by the teenage girl who could wield

5

Annie Oakley's height in feet (1.5 m).

- Born Phoebe Ann Mosey, 1860–1926.
- Famous for being a sharpshooter.
- Featured in the musical *Annie Get Your Gun.*

a rifle so well. She started traveling with performance groups using the stage name Annie Oakley. In 1885, she joined Buffalo Bill's show and traveled the world.

Annie Oakley's fame continued in films and plays loosely based on her life. Songs from the 1946 musical *Annie Get Your Gun* are still big hits. People were drawn to the story of this talented sharpshooter and trailblazer for women.

BETSY ROSS STORY CAPTURES AMERICA'S FANCY

Betsy Ross was a seamstress in Philadelphia. After her husband died in the American Revolution, she took over the family's upholstery business. Legend has it that Ross's busy hands sewed the first American flag. According to the popular story, George Washington visited Ross's home in 1776. Washington asked her to sew a flag for the new nation.

He showed her a rough design and then used some of her suggestions to make a new sketch. Ross suggested using five-point stars instead of six-point stars. Then she stitched the first flag in her back parlor.

Ross's grandson, William J. Canby, first told this story in 1870. Canby

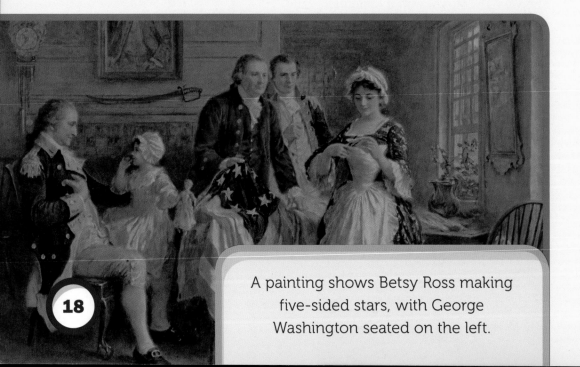

A painting shows Betsy Ross making five-sided stars, with George Washington seated on the left.

said this story had been passed down through his family. But no evidence has been found that Ross designed the flag. Historians do not think it is a true story. Still, Americans have been telling it for more than a century. Many like the idea of Ross as a plucky widow who ran her own business. They enjoy the thought of Washington himself making the request. The story has come to represent ideas of patriotism and public service.

In 1893, Charles Weisberger painted a picture of Betsy Ross.

Tourists can visit the Betsy Ross house in Philadelphia, Pennsylvania.

In it, Ross is showing the flag to George Washington. The painting became very popular and drew more attention to the story.

13
Number of stars and stripes on the first flag approved by the Continental Congress in 1777.

- Born Elizabeth Griscom, 1752–1836.
- Story first told by William J. Canby, 1870.
- Depicted in Charles Weisberger's painting, *The Birth of Our Nation's Flag*, 1893.

STAR-SPANGLED BANNER

Another famous seamstress is Mary Pickersgill. She made the flag that became known as the Star-Spangled Banner after it inspired the national anthem. It flew over Fort McHenry during the War of 1812. Pickersgill's flag measured 30 by 42 feet (9 by 13 m) and weighed approximately 150 pounds (70 kg).

JAMES BECKWOURTH SPINS YARNS ABOUT MOUNTAIN LIFE

James Beckwourth made himself a legend. As a fur trapper in the Rocky Mountains, he often told stories around campfires. And most of these stories were about himself. He was known to exaggerate his strength and skills. In one of his stories, he used only an ax to fight off a large group of armed men. Another time, he ran into a bear's cave with just a knife and killed it.

Eventually the African-American trapper told his stories to a journalist, Thomas Bonner. Bonner made them into a book, *The Life and Adventures of James P. Beckwourth, Mountaineer, Scout, Pioneer and Chief of the Crow Nation of Indians.* It was published in 1856. Soon, many people were enjoying Beckwourth's stories.

Many of Beckwourth's adventures took place in the Sierra Nevada Mountains.

At least some of Beckwourth's tales were true. He did live among the Crow Indians for six years. And in about 1850, Beckwourth discovered a low pass through the Sierra Nevada Mountains. Settlers used the pass to cross from Nevada into California after gold was discovered there.

5,221

Elevation in feet (1,591 m) of Beckwourth Pass.

- Born as James Beckwith, 1798–1867.
- Fur trapper and storyteller who spread legends about himself.
- Collection of his stories published in 1856.

A 1994 stamp featured James Beckwourth.

USA 29

CASEY JONES BECOMES HERO OF THE RAILROAD

Railroad engineer Casey Jones was always on time. Folks set their clocks by his train, the Cannonball Special. Casey's real name was Jonathan Luther Jones. People called him Casey after his hometown, Cayce, Kentucky. On April 30, 1900, Jones died when his train crashed into a train car that was stuck on the track. But his heroic actions saved the lives of every other person on the train. He spent his last seconds trying to apply the brakes to slow the train down. He blew the whistle to warn of the crash and yelled at his

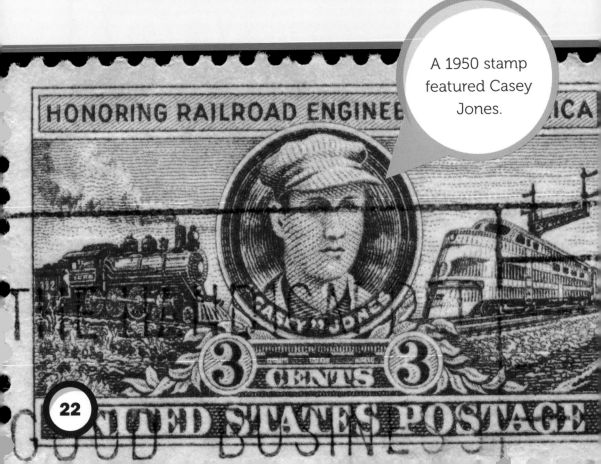

A 1950 stamp featured Casey Jones.

HONORING RAILROAD ENGINEER
"CASEY" JONES
3 CENTS 3
UNITED STATES POSTAGE

assistant, Sim Webb, to jump from the train. Webb survived.

A friend of Jones, Wallace Saunders, wrote a song for him after his death. "The Ballad of Casey Jones" told the story of Jones's heroic actions the day he died. Railroad workers began to sing it along Casey Jones's old railroad line. One of them passed it along to a pair of professional songwriters.

Soon different versions were being performed on stage or recorded. In the 1930s, the story was retold in a book, a movie, and a radio series.

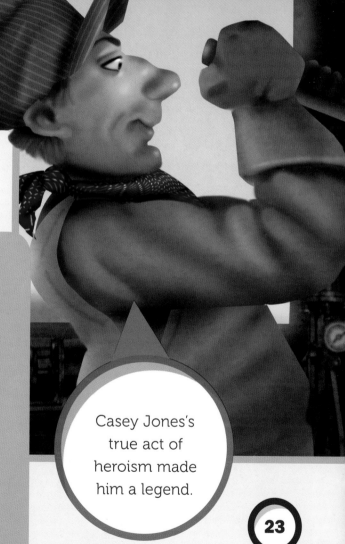

1 million

Approximate number of copies sold of different versions of "The Ballad of Casey Jones" by 1914.

- Born as Jonathan Luther Jones, 1863–1901.
- Worked on the Illinois Central Railroad.
- Remembered in "The Ballad of Casey Jones."

Casey Jones's true act of heroism made him a legend.

MOLLY PITCHER REPRESENTS WOMEN OF THE REVOLUTION

According to legend, Molly Pitcher helped colonial soldiers during the American Revolution. During the Battle of Monmouth in 1778, she carried pitchers of water to cool the cannons and give the soldiers a drink. When her husband was wounded, she took over his cannon. She fired it for the rest of the battle.

Some historians think Molly Pitcher was actually Mary Hays McCauly.

The grave of Mary Hays McCauly, thought to be Molly Pitcher, is in Carlisle, Pennsylvania.

Military records show McCauly's husband fought in the Revolution. The state of Pennsylvania paid her for some sort of military service, but records do not say what she actually did. Margaret Corbin also has been identified as Molly Pitcher. Corbin fought at the Battle of Fort Washington in 1776. Records show the military considered her a soldier.

Others think that Molly Pitcher was not one person.

Rather, she represented all women who helped during the American Revolution. From the 1850s, songs, art, books, and films have told Molly Pitcher's tale.

$40

Amount the government paid Mary Hays McCauly per year for her services during the American Revolution.

- Molly Pitcher was possibly based on Mary Hays McCauly, 1754–1832.
- May have helped at the Battle of Monmouth, June 28, 1778.
- Also known as Captain Molly.

A drawing shows Molly Pitcher at the Battle of Monmouth.

12

BRER RABBIT OVERCOMES OPPONENTS WITH TRICKERY

Brer Rabbit was a popular character in African-American tales. He was good at outsmarting other animals. In one story, Brer Rabbit is caught in a trap. He tricks Brer Fox into taking his place. In another, the rabbit falls down a well. He tricks the fox into saving him. These trickster tales were often very funny. But they also spoke to the inequality experienced by the people who told them. The character represented the idea that someone who was weaker could overcome a stronger enemy through cleverness.

Brer Rabbit stories were first told in Africa. When Africans were enslaved by American plantation owners, the slaves continued the tradition of telling these stories. The storytellers used places or experiences from their day-to-day lives in the tales. Slaves had very little freedom and lived in harsh conditions. Most were not allowed to learn to read or write. They could be punished for complaining about their lives. When the slaves told Brer Rabbit stories, the animal characters often stood for the storytellers and the smart ways they learned to survive.

In 1879, journalist Joel Chandler Harris started recording some of the Brer Rabbit tales. He had heard these tales as a child. Harris published them in books beginning in 1881. Now, Brer Rabbit has fans around the world. Stories have been printed in more than 30 languages.

THINK ABOUT IT

Oral storytelling is an important part of many cultures. Why do you think this is? What can stories tell us about a culture?

8

Books of Brer Rabbit stories written by Joel Chandler Harris.

- Tales have their beginnings in African folklore.
- Told by African-American slaves.
- First published in the *Atlanta Constitution* in 1879.

A children's book illustration from the 1800s shows Brer Rabbit talking to younger rabbits.

FACT SHEET

- Several organizations exist to study and preserve cultural folklore. The American Folklore Society was founded in 1888. Members study folklore from around the world. The American Folklife Center was created in 1976 as part of the Library of Congress. Its purpose is to research, preserve, and educate people about American folklore.

- Songs are popular ways to tell and retell myths and legends. Many of the stories in this book have songs connected to them. The Library of Congress has the largest collection of folk songs in the United States.

- Some American legends feature patriotic heroes, such as Betsy Ross or Molly Pitcher. These stories express popular American values, such as honesty or service.

- Many stories have been told about President George Washington to portray him as a hero. According to one made-up story, Washington cut down a cherry tree. When his father asked him about it, he admitted to cutting it down, saying, "I cannot tell a lie."

- In 1994, the US Postal Service issued twenty 29-cent stamps featuring Legends of the West. Annie Oakley and Jim Beckwourth were among those honored.

- Many statues and sculptures feature characters from myths and legends. Klamath, California, boasts a 49-foot (14.9-m) tall statue of Paul Bunyan. An 18-foot (5.5-m) statue of Paul Bunyan is on display in Bemidji, Minnesota.

- Disney has produced several short films on American legends. *The Legend of Johnny Appleseed* came out in 1948. In 1950, *The Brave Engineer* told the story of Casey Jones. The short movie *Paul Bunyan* was released in 1958. *John Henry* came out in 2000.

GLOSSARY

chantey
A song sung by sailors.

enslaved
Forced to do work for no pay as
a slave.

exaggerate
To describe something as larger or
greater than it really is.

frontier
A region on the edge of settled or
developed territory.

legend
A story based on a real person
or events.

logger
A person who chops down trees.

orchard
A place where fruit trees are planted.

scout
A member of a military unit who goes
ahead to gather information.

settler
A person who goes to live in a new
place where there are few people.

sharpshooter
Someone who is skilled at shooting
at a target with a gun.

supernatural
Unable to be explained by science or
the laws of nature.

symbol
Something that stands for
something else.

trapper
A person who hunted animals for
their skins or furs.

values
Ideas about principles or traits that
are important.

FOR MORE INFORMATION

Books

Osborne, Mary Pope. *American Tall Tales*. New York: Knopf Books for Young Readers, 2013.

York, M. J. *Casey Jones*. North Mankato, MN: The Child's World, 2013.

York, M. J. *Johnny Appleseed*. North Mankato, MN: The Child's World, 2013.

York, M. J. *Paul Bunyan*. North Mankato, MN: The Child's World, 2013.

York, M. J. *Pecos Bill*. North Mankato, MN: The Child's World, 2013.

Websites

American Folklore
www.americanfolklore.net

Smithsonian Center for Folklife and Cultural America
www.folklife.si.edu

World of Tales: North American Folktales
www.worldoftales.com/North_American_folktales.html

INDEX

About the Author

Anita Yasuda is the author of more than 80 books for children. She has written biographies, books about science and social studies, and chapter books. She lives in Huntington Beach, California.

READ MORE FROM 12-STORY LIBRARY

Every 12-Story Library book is available in many formats, including Amazon Kindle and Apple iBooks. For more information, visit your device's store or 12StoryLibrary.com.